THE
EVERLASTING
HUNGER
FOR
IMPROVEMENT

THE EVERLASTING HUNGER FOR IMPROVEMENT

The Hunger for Improvement Never Ends

JORDAN O. SALZANO

Library of Congress Control Number:		2020924203
ISBN:	Hardcover	978-1-6641-4566-5
	Softcover	978-1-6641-4565-8
	eBook	978-1-6641-4564-1

Print information available on the last page.

Rev. date: 12/18/2020

To order additional copies of this book, contact:
Xlibris
844-714-8691
www.Xlibris.com
Orders@Xlibris.com
823027

Contents

Dedication

This book is dedicated to those in my life who I have benefited from being associated with—and for those who have the same mentality I do: *to never stop improving.*

To those who have not yet found the answers they're looking for in the process that they're engulfed in.

And of course, to my family, for being the best source of support there is out there. I would not be where I am today without them.

Thank you, all.

Introduction:
My Desire to Write this Book,
and a True Story

I have been interested in the concept of motivation ever since I was a young kid. Let me share a bit about my journey, and why this topic is so personal—and passionate—for me.

My love for motivation and passion for innovation in my life has erupted ever since I started playing sports. I used to do karate, and shortly after that, I started playing ice hockey and soccer. To add onto that, in high school, I also picked up tennis, which is something that I have developed a great love for. I have played other various sports in my lifetime, as I am an athletic person.

Of course, with sports, there has to be some type of motivation to perform, because without the energy to want to play, it is almost inevitable that you will not get the greatest results—not just individually, but possibly as a team as well. Every person is vital to a team, and if one piece of the puzzle in fact doesn't fit, it can impact the outcome—as well as the dynamic.

Years ago, I would go on YouTube and watch videos of compilations of some of the most famous speeches, from present day public speakers to lines from inspiring movies, etc. I loved watching really anything that would light a flame in not just me, but other viewers, too. I began to notice the types of videos that got the most notice, and I saw that they often were very positive and uplifting. The comments on these videos also influenced me, as just about all of them said how impacting and uplifting the video(s) were. Comments ranged from, "I feel so motivated now," to, "This helped me wake up this morning and go to school," etc.

So, how did this habit of watching positive videos relate to sports? I usually watched these when I would work out or before a sports game or practice—you know, to get pumped! I'd watch compilations on YouTube of athletes talking about their grinds and stories of how they reached their current levels. I would even listen to these videos while walking into the hockey rink—mind you not even warming up yet—because they gave me a sense of confidence, and my adrenaline would start to pump.

It was an amazing feeling, and to put the icing on the cake, I was also playing a sport I loved. When we would first step on to the ice for a game or practice, the words I'd listened to prior ran around in my head, and I would even say them under my breath while I was stickhandling or something (I often loved to stickhandle to start practice, and still do to this day). For those who don't know, stickhandling is moving the puck from side to side on your blade of your stick, or the bottom of it. Think of it as dribbling, like in basketball. It's dribbling, except the puck is not supposed to come off the ice and you're using a stick instead of your hands.

Anyway, I would repeat the words over and over again, and I also would do this when I was actually playing in the game. When the words came to mind, I could feel myself skating harder and going a bit faster, like someone was pushing me.

Something that I have learned not just from these videos, but just from being a student of life, is that improvement is absolutely necessary to get through this journey of life that we all are in. My coaches would tell me that my work ethic to improve was amazing and that I was a "work horse." This, I could see, inspired my teammates too. They would start the drill, I would do it, and when it was their turn to go again, they would go even harder than they had the first time. I mean I can't read minds, but something would always tell me that there was a reason that they were going harder—to try to work harder than me. And as much as I have always strived to be top notch, it was good to see this, because I felt like a great example. My teammates would push themselves so that we could perform better as a team. In that process, they would also be improving themselves.

With that being said, there have been times when I would improve insidiously at something—gradually getting better—and other times when I would improve at a faster, steadier rate. Everybody has their strengths and weaknesses, so that concept played a huge role in my improvement too. The things that I was subpar at, for example math, would take me a lot longer than most of my classmates to understand. That is still the case to this day. However, when it came to something that I was above par at, such as playing the piano, I would learn to play a part of a song faster than the people who surrounded me.

I have learned that as long as you're improving, you're going the right way. *Up is the way to go.* By constantly improving, doors have opened for me that I honestly never dreamed of entering before. If it weren't for my improvement in grammar and punctuation throughout the years, for example, I wouldn't have been able to write this book and inspire you. Improvement is what led me here. I fell in love with the process of improving and realized how important it is for us to develop a passion for the climb of life. Life is something that all of us have in common, and it involves a gradual process of improvement: from birth to older age. If you want to achieve greatness, or even a lick of improvement, you must be willing to do the hard work—and enjoy the process when you can.

When I was in elementary school, I got diagnosed with Asperger's syndrome. For those who don't know, Asperger's syndrome is a disorder on the ASD (Autism Spectrum Disorder) that includes disability in social interaction/social communication, alongside excessive interest in one or more things and repetitive behavior. An example of something that a person with Asperger's would experience is a huge interest in something, but when introduced to other new things, they find it hard to want to engage in that change or new subject. An example of this in my life is my excessive interest in Elvis Presley (1935-1977). For those who know me, you know that his name is in my daily vocabulary. Often, because I am mighty interested in him and really appreciate listening to him, I find it hard to want to listen to other types of music. Now don't get me wrong; I do like various other artists. For example, I enjoy Johnny Cash as well. However, Elvis is someone that I listen to daily and can never get enough of. I even like to bring him up in conversations. It's like an obsession, and even though it's not a bad obsession, I know that I have to work on controlling it—because it is harder for me, a person with Asperger's, to do so.

An upside of Asperger's, however, is that the integrity to perform and work hard is top notch. An example of this in my life was my work ethic with ice hockey. I was relentless on and off the ice and everybody around me knew it. I worked my tail off even if we were doing an easy drill, or something or the sort.

Due to Asperger's, I would often run into barriers that prevented me from interacting with society as an average person would. I have grown up the vast majority of my life, up until high school, finding it very hard to make friends and talk to people whilst having a normal conversation. I was usually the one who sat alone at lunch or the one who was told I couldn't join in a fun game with classmates, by my classmates. For example in middle school, when in Physical Education class, my classmates would pick me last if we were choosing teams to play a game. I would usually just be a "sub"—or not even get a chance to play. My classmates would look at me and whisper to each other—and laugh.

Another example of a lunch situation, throughout my first twelve years of education, is when I would sit down, and whoever was sitting there would say, "Someone is sitting there." Meanwhile, minutes later, I would look over, and no one was sitting there.

Also, various times I would sit down and people would just get up and leave.

You know, at a young age, this sometimes felt like the end of the world. I felt so embarrassed. My face would get so red, and I would be on the verge of tears at times. Mind you, this didn't just happen once. This happened multiple times, not just in sports, but also just with friend groups and other situations. I was always the outcast, and it felt horrible. I felt like I didn't belong with anyone. Being lonely is one of the worst feelings in the world, and for years, this was a norm for me, just about every day.

This stuff still happens to this day. People treat me differently, because I'm not like them. I get "shoved" out of friend groups, and friends turn their backs on me, and I sit there and wonder what I did wrong. Let me tell you, it definitely does mess with my mind. It is not a fun thing to deal with. It doesn't happen nearly as often it used to, but the pattern still lingers on.

My barriers have led me to show a great amount of immaturity, which turned a lot of people off from me. For example, I would walk into a room and start laughing and talking to people, meanwhile everyone in the room was not in the mood to be on the level of positivity that I was on. I could not see that. People would wonder what was wrong with me. They would yell at me, and honestly, I wouldn't even know what the big deal was. Imagine not knowing what you're doing wrong—and people screaming at you for it? It made me feel absolutely terrible. You know the expression "read the room"? Well I did not know what this meant. I was horrible at it. Even to this day, I still sort of struggle with it.

As a result of all this isolation and tension I felt at school, I wanted to make more friends to escape these feelings. I desperately wanted to do my best to change my situation. However, I didn't know what to change until I found mentors to help me. I saw many therapists and practiced social situations at home with my family. For example, my parents would ask me to walk into a room, and they would be "classmates" and act a certain way. I would have to try to read the vibe of the room for a few seconds, and I would then assimilate to that vibe. This helped me with my "reading the room" situation. The duration of this training and learning about how to work through these challenges lasted many years, and it was a lot of work. But let me tell you, it paid off greatly. I have gotten so much better at my social skills. I've learned how to act accordingly in certain situations that I lacked skill in, and as a result, my maturity and comfort in my own skin has developed greatly.

Due to all of the therapy and such that I would practice, I have seen blessings far outside of what I could imagine. I was able to make such amazing friends that are so understanding—and some who I can call very close. Back in my younger years, I would've never been able to make these friends. That's why I didn't. I didn't possess the skills to do so. But my development finally hit a peak in high school, and due to the fact that I honed the necessary skills to do well socially, I made unbreakable bonds with some people whom I am so blessed to know.

Now don't get me wrong, I do have more work to do. However, I am looking forward to it because it is all part of the process. Why should I stop now? There are never-ending plateaus to break!

All of these experiences have equipped me with tools to make conversations with many people every day—in the classroom, on the sports field, at lunch, etc. I have a lot more friends than I did, because of my *hunger to improve* socially—my desire to become better at socializing. If I had never seen a therapist or practiced social situations, I would've never evolved into as good of a light as I am in now.

It's amazing to see what can happen in a period of time, with dedication to get better. I give thanks to my *Hunger for Improvement (which I often call HFI)* for getting me to where I am now and for giving me the desire to never stop improving in life!

Now I want to share how you can develop a *Hunger for Improvement*— to take your life to the next level. Are you ready?

Get your seatbelts on. The light is about to change to green.

Chapter 1

What Does This Hunger Mean?

The Merriam-Webster's dictionary definition of 'hunger" is *a weakened condition brought about by prolonged lack of food.* When you are hungry, you start paying attention to your hunger, and most of the time, you can't stop thinking of food. Food is all you care about when you get hungry. Things that can contribute to the intensity of that hunger are amazing smells from local restaurants, images of food, somebody talking about their favorite dish, etc. If you're extremely hungry, you might drop whatever you're doing and literally go on a mission to find something that will satisfy your hunger. Once you eat and finish your meal or snack, you will feel better and can focus on other things that are thrown at you daily.

Running on empty is not a good feeling at all. Just like with a car, if you are running low on gas, you need to find a gas station as soon as possible, or else your car will stop working due to lack of energy to keep it going. The same is true with your hunger.

As it is referred to all around the world, when someone says they're hungry, most of the time they are referring to hunger for *food*. They are craving a burger, ice cream, a certain snack, etc.—anything they can eat to satisfy that feeling.

But what if I said that there was a different type of hunger—a hunger that doesn't have to do with food? You're probably saying, "What?" or are confused, because you've never heard of such a thing. Hunger means you want to eat, right? Isn't that what it has always meant since the dawn of time?

Yeah, that's right. But this type of hunger has nothing to do with anything physical, or anything that you can place in your hand. This hunger doesn't require you to pay with the American dollar in order to satisfy your stomach. This hunger does not come from your stomach whatsoever.

To add onto that, this hunger lasts more than a few hours. It lasts as long as it is needed, which can be weeks, months, even years. Or maybe even a lifetime—*everlasting.*

A hunger that lasts longer than a few hours to a day? What?! That's crazy talk.

Yes, it is crazy talk, but there are reasons why this type of talk is indeed *a good crazy.*

Without this type of hunger, it is hard to get through life. And the name of this hunger is the *Hunger for Improvement* (which as I mentioned, I sometimes call HFI).

That's the name. If you're wondering what it means, it's all in the name, *Hunger for Improvement.* Merriam-Webster defines improvement as *an instance of such improvement, or something that enhances value and/or excellence.* So an example of an improvement would be learning to read or ride a bike. At the start, you didn't know what to do. The book and the bike probably looked mighty complex to you. Once you started to learn to read and ride, however, you got better and better at the tasks given. When applying yourself to such activities, by practicing consistently, you eventually made it look so easy. It's like eating a piece of cake now.

But why is it that simple? It wasn't easy when you first started, remember? It was the hardest thing in the world at first.

I will reveal the secret to you. The secret is *you improved yourself.* You improved in reading and riding, and now can do them with your eyes closed (metaphorically). Your improvement led to these accomplishments. If it weren't for your efforts at improvement, you would still be struggling.

To add to that, the beginning of every single thing you do in life is ALWAYS going to be the hardest. You won't ever look at something brand new, something that you simply cannot familiarize yourself with, and instantly master the craft. For example, let's just say you buy a state-of-the-art new laptop. You come home from the store one day with the box that contains the new, prized possession and other accessories. Now you may know how to open the box, but what happens after that? I mean, the laptop won't come assembled, plugged in, and optimized for your use all by itself. If there were nothing to guide you through the process of setting it up, i.e. an instruction manual, you would be lost. You are a new user to this model of laptop, and that means that you need guidance. You're a beginner. You are BEGINning to master everything there is to know about this computer.

The beginning is a platform that is needed to start your journey on. You can't start on thin air.

So now let's put *hunger* and *improvement* together. You know how you improved on bike riding and book reading? Well, if you think about it, you already had the Hunger for Improvement. If you didn't want to get better at those things and didn't care to know how, you wouldn't even have known where to start with riding and reading.

So, listen here. You *did* have that hunger inside of you, even without knowing it. And now, since you are older and wiser, you can apply that hunger to things in life that will actually bring you to *the best version of yourself you can be.*

What I mean by "best version of yourself" is you will become the best *you* that you can possibly be. You will showcase all of your inner beauty and show the world *the real you.* Nobody else can become the best version of you, because their name isn't yours, and they can't control your life. You are you; they are them. There's only one you in this world. There's not even another you in another country. So why not make *you* the best, since you are a valuable original?

Gold is gold. Accept the reality that you are unique and precious. You bring an element to the table of society.

So now you know what the Hunger for Improvement is. When you have a certain desire, or a dream that you wish to achieve, you'll do anything to reach it, right? You've already proven that you can do this, since you are reading this book.

You've learned many skills in life that you now take for granted. You did so because you had a drive in you to get better and accomplish a goal. That's the Hunger for Improvement.

You already have the Hunger for Improvement. Now you just need to become aware of it—and tap into it for even more greatness. I bet that one or more times in your life, you have worked to get somewhere. No matter if you made it to your planned destination or not, you had that Hunger to Improve. So, you can say that you had it.

Nice! Bravo!

And I bet that you'll put in the extra hours to help launch yourself to become phenomenal in whatever it is you want to become. Take a minute or so and ask yourself this question with full honesty: is there something that you want right now? I'm not talking about a food or something like that. I am talking about a certain accomplishment. You may even want to put in the work to get there. If so, you know what the definition of that *desire* is now. You recognize that *hunger.*

You may have the desire now, but will it last? If so, for how long? Time will tell. It's your job to keep that hunger "in taste" for as long as you can. Just like you may have a craving for ice cream or your favorite snack, if you want something that badly… if you want that craving to lead you to success… the Hunger to Improve will play a big role in getting you to the top.

I will give you one example of when I had the Hunger for Improvement in my lifetime so far. When I was around six years old, I fell in love with the sport of ice hockey. Now I was quite young at the time, so I had not yet thought of the phrase "Hunger for Improvement." All I knew how to do was have fun on the ice, make friends with my teammates, and always do my best.

Very shortly after I commenced playing hockey, I dreamed and envisioned myself getting far with the sport— for example, playing tier one during my youth years, then getting a chance to play division one in college, and hopefully professionally. Once these thoughts started popping into my head, I knew that the only way to even get a chance to play at these levels was to work for it.

Luckily for me, hard work just came naturally. It still does. In school, even at such a young age, I never settled for an F on a test. Hard work was what I knew. I was never "talented"—where the results would come naturally. Everything that I was and am didn't come easy.

That also included ice hockey. I never went "easy" during a drill. I knew that the only way to improve was to push myself. Even if I would fall, whatever, I'd get back up and keep going. That showed coaches that I cared about improvement. Have you ever been recognized for your effort, even when you might not have had the most skills?

In the process of trying something I wasn't immediately good at, I learned why falling—or failing—is not something to fear, but is part of the process. I have had coaches tell me, "I would rather you fall a thousand times, than never fall and go 50 percent at it." That is something I hope sticks in your mind, because often people think of falling as embarrassing. It can be for a bit of time, but would you rather be embarrassed for a few minutes—or for years because you were afraid of being embarrassed for a short time? What I mean by that is, would you rather look like you don't know what you're doing for a little time, feel the embarrassment, and move on? Or would you rather not take that chance, because you're afraid of embarrassment— leading to never mastering the skill, and as a result looking like you don't know what you're doing for years? No right or wrong answer. It's up to you. What would you rather?

I would much rather feel the shame for a few minutes rather than feel it for an eternity. I would rather take on humility for a few minutes rather than an eternity.

Find your passion and get ready to execute. Be willing to take risks and fall to get to where you are meant to be. If you are as serious as I was about improving myself in order to get to the next level, then you will accept that the Hunger for Improvement is vital for your success. Make yourself remain hungry for your goal. Get so familiar with it that you can taste it.

Now let's get into detail on how to pursue this Hunger for Improvement. Make sure your seat is comfortable! Here we go.

Autobots, let's roll out.

Self-Reflection Rest Stop

Welcome to the self-reflection rest stop! At the end of each chapter, this rest stop will be provided for you to come face to face with yourself and answer a few questions with full honesty. Take as long as you need to answer these questions—there is no time limit. This is your time. Park your mind, step outside for a bit, stretch if you need to, and begin when you're ready.

The objective of the self-reflection rest stop is to come out of each chapter with a clear mind on what you are good at and what you may need to improve on. That's what self-reflection is all about!

1. What do you really want to do with your life? If you know the answer, are you willing to do whatever it takes to reach that goal?

2. When was the last time you believe you had the Hunger for Improvement? What did it make you feel like? What did you do about it?

3. Would you rather just stick to your talent—or work hard to break through that plateau of talent?

    Would you rather be considered talented—or a hard worker?

4. Do you believe that you can apply that physical hunger for food into mental hunger? Do you think you can tap into your passion and feel starved mentally for that thing you want to achieve?

5. How do you usually embody humility? Are you satisfied with your level of humility, or do you wish to handle it a different way? If so, what is that way?

Chapter 2

How Do I Develop This Hunger?

When you have not eaten in hours, you start to get hungry. Your stomach starts to grumble like a volcano, and you don't feel the same way you did when your stomach was satisfied. Sometimes—or even most of the time, to be fair—you cannot simply get your mind off the food that is awaiting your consumption. Food becomes a medicine to help you focus on your daily activities, and without that relief that comes with consuming it, you can't focus, no matter how important those tasks are.

Why wouldn't you want medicine, if it is the trick to help you get back on your feet? When you aren't feeling well, don't you want to feel better? Don't you want that Tylenol or other relief to treat your ailment? If you want to feel sick, you're crazy, honey. However, if you want to feel that way, all I can say in that situation is *you do you*.

So, the bottom line is, when you're hungry, food is the ideal medicine. When you aren't feeling very well, antibiotics and rest may be the best medicine.

On the contrary, for your Hunger to Improve, the medicine is not physical. As I've said, you cannot hold it in the palm of your hand. For that reason, it's definitely different than the normal discomfort reliever. The medicine for your Hunger for Improvement...... drumroll please.......

is PASSION! Your passion is what gets you working through that Hunger for Improvement. Your passion is what you need to keep that Hunger for Improvement going—even as you are fed along the way. That passion is what creates the Hunger for Improvement, day after day. It's the key to the everlasting will to succeed.

You might be saying, "Wait, don't you not want to be hungry anymore? Why would you want passion if it will just make the hunger last longer?"

Well it is pretty simple, actually. Your passion is what keeps you going after your goal, right? The desire for your passion leads you to put in the extra work to be the best you can be. And that work will get you to your destination.

Once that destination is reached, you may not feel the need to go any further. If you are at peace with your position when you reach your desired destination, you won't feel as hungry to keep moving. It's the same thing way food; you are hungry, until you consume something. Then you're A-okay, ready to go on with your day—ready to put your mind to the tasks that life throws at you again.

Always remember that you can become satisfied with your work at any time, however. You can go halfway and feel at ease with yourself. When you eat something, you may only eat one portion of it, be halfway full, and feel fine with that. It depends on how hungry you are. The process of satisfying hunger isn't the same for everyone, so it's okay to take a break halfway or when you aren't completely full yet.

Snap, just like the hunger that comes back the next morning even if we ate a big meal the night before, the Hunger for Improvement can stay active. Feeding it each day helps build your appetite (or passion) for bigger challenges.

Just like we can adjust our diet over time to be more satisfying and healthy—reaping the long-term benefits—we can also adjust how we live our lives, day by day, to satisfy our Hunger for Improvement.

Many people on this Earth have a passion, no matter what that passion is. If you do not have a certain passion at this moment, don't worry. You have a lifetime to figure it out.

Now a passion typically does not just appear one day, like you don't just wake up one morning and have a passion for something that you've never done before. For example, if you've never played or watched football before, you likely won't wake up one day and love the sport. You have to experience the game in order to get a feel for how you like it. It's like that with food, too. You can't say that you like or dislike a food if you've never tried it. You have to taste it in order to have an opinion on it. Even though I'm sure some of us just look at a type of food and say "no," your official opinion doesn't come into play until you actually taste it.

So, say you watch football one day, and you enjoy the tenacity of the sport and how it's played. You claim that you want to try out the sport to get a feel for it, or to even feel like your favorite NFL players/player. You buy cleats, a helmet, etc. You go to a local clinic over the weekend or during the week. You continue to go every week, and you fall in love with the game. You start dreaming about how you can possibly make it to the NFL (National Football League)—or even any college team.

To reach those goals, you know that you must work to get there. Next, you start looking up ways to practice your skills and apply them either daily or weekly. You may study on the internet or get advice from a pioneer of the sport.

Suddenly, all you can think about is football—and your hopes of making it big one day. When you reach this point—when the drive to get better consumes you— congratulations! You have created yourself *a passion.*

Now, in order to keep this passion alive, you must play the sport—and do your best every time you step on the field. And HAVE FUN with it! Please do not pressure yourself to be perfect with every play and drill, because that is impossible. Passion is great and all, but you have to have fun.

In fact, that fun can make your passion stronger. Who has a passion for something they don't enjoy? Nobody I know does.

There have been times when I have pressured myself too much with my passion, and every time I messed up, I thought as if my career was over. Sad but true. I only focused on what was weak with myself, and it made me crack. If I did something right, it was never good enough. I self-assessed, which was an important thing to do, but I did it to an unhealthy extreme.

For example, in ice hockey when I would miss the net, I would slam my stick and get so angry that I couldn't focus on what I was doing next. A wave of embarrassment would flow over me, and I let my failure get to me terribly. Even after a practice, I would keep thinking about it, and I would sometimes even have that same unnecessary burden with me for the next couple of days. Literally over missing the net…. in a practice. How stupid does that sound?

I loved hockey, but to a point of nauseum—where I could never mess up. Honestly, looking back at it, I kept saying to myself that I loved hockey, and the reason why I felt disappointed in myself was also because I loved it so much.

That's not the case. I wasn't in love with the process at that time. I just wanted to be *perfect.*

Part of loving something is loving the ups and downs, and I loved only one part and not the other. I only enjoyed the times when I was succeeding.

Do not end up like that. You have to love what you do first. Your love will lead to you wanting to do more of it, and that can lead into a passion. Love and passion are intertwined; however only one of those things starts the process. The starter is love. If the love isn't there, the passion isn't there. When the passion isn't there, the work doesn't get done. LOVE what you do!

Love begins with liking something. With getting introduced to it, no matter your age. When I first saw hockey, I liked everything I saw about it. When I started playing, I loved the skills I was learning. I felt like I was in a different world, a great one. I felt freedom from my everyday stresses. I loved getting onto the ice with my team. Over time, my love grew into a deep passion—and my skills sharpened too.

Skills will come with time, but your love for what you're doing is most important of all. That love will spark your passion.

Just as a warning, be cautious, for there will be many bumps in the road. There will be times when you will want to step away from whatever you're doing. That's normal. It happens to all of us. But if you really love what you're doing, you will come back to it at some point.

Love is tested at the most troubled times. It wouldn't make sense for love to be tested at good times, because if things kept going your way, why would your love for whatever it is you're doing lessen? Everything looks good for you during easy times, and it's therefore easy to keep moving. The true test comes when your commitment is challenged.

For example, say two people who are in a relationship get into an argument. If the love is tight between the two, no matter how long it may take to talk to one another again, they will work things out and start anew. If the love isn't as tight, or isn't tight at all, they possibly will never speak to each other—carrying that burden of blame towards their significant other for as long as time. Or one of the people, or even both possibly, will even deep down know or believe that it was his/her fault that the relationship took a dive, but be unwilling to admit it.

Do you see how this all connects? Your love and passion for something is what keeps you in the game. Love leads to passion, which leads to hard work, which leads to opportunities, which leads to experience, which leads to lessons learned, which leads to fixes in behaviors and habits, which leads to success. I know that may seem like a lot to swallow and process, but let me tell you, it is candid. In order to receive and work with the Hunger for Improvement, you must have a passion for whatever it is you are doing. There's no hunger without passion or drive. Everything connects, just like a puzzle.

Here is a real-life example of what I am talking about. Here is how I developed my Hunger to Improve in ice hockey: *I found the sport.* It was on TV all the time in my house growing up, usually all New York Rangers' games, because my family bleeds blue. All of that watching introduced me to my future love, and I wanted to try it. I wanted to feel like some of my favorite Rangers players, for example Dan Girardi and Derek Stepan. Not just Rangers players, but also players from other teams that I knew at the time: Sidney Crosby, Jonathan Toews, Erik Karlsson, Alex Ovechkin, to name a few. I wanted to skate like Sidney Crosby, shoot like Alex Ovechkin, have the great senses of Jonathan Toews, and make amazing plays and have the vision of Erik Karlsson, etc. I thought of how cool it would be to do what they did. It is pretty cool stuff to watch and do, even if you're not a hockey fan.

I started skating and took skating lessons. I did everything under the sun to get familiar with the sport in person. I played in house leagues, or rec leagues, to start my days of competing. As the days went on, my dreams of playing at cream-of-the-crop levels infused into my head more and more. These thoughts became engraved into my mind, and they barely ever escaped.

I took it upon myself to work as hard as I possibly could, absolutely relentlessly, for a chance to come face to face with these roads of opportunity that just lay alive in my mind. I was *starving* to make my dream become a reality. I was never satisfied at night unless I'd done some sort of training to better myself.

I found something, I introduced myself to it, I fell in love with it, my passion grew, and therefore my work ethic grew! It felt extravagant at first, even though it was mighty hard.

Skating is tough. It took me months to be able to skate on my own without holding onto something. Now I can skate—and contribute to a successful team—because I introduced myself to something, fell in love with it, grew a passion for it, and the work ethic took over from there.

I played at a prep school due to my developed passion. I worked my rear end off to achieve a goal that, for a large portion of my life, I would never have even considered having the confidence to achieve.

Everybody has that ability to dream about something; it is so easy to do so. But there are those people who just sleep with those dreams, and then there are those who want to put their dreams physically in front of them.

It takes guts to *get up* and *get after* your dream. Are you willing to sacrifice your down time to become the best version of yourself? Are you ready to become the greatest you can possibly be at something? That's your own choice to make.

Self-Reflection Rest Stop

Welcome back! Time for some more self-reflection! Time to potentially become a better you!

1. What is your main passion at the moment? For how long has this been in your life?

2. What is the best moment that happened to you with this passion? How about the worst? What did the worst moment do for you, meaning how did you deal with it the minute after it happened?

3. What is the highest level of pressure that you have ever reached with your passion? How badly did it overwhelm you? Looking back, did you handle it as well as you wanted to?

4. Who or what helped you through the darkest of times with your passion? Have you really engraved those strategies for coping with the nauseating pressure into your mind and applied yourself to them, or have you just let the advice go in one ear and out the other?

5. Has there ever come a time when you stepped away from your passion for a little while? Did you go back to it? If so, what would you consider to be the main driving? Do you still think about that driving force to this day?

Chapter 3

Don't Lie to Yourself!

Everybody on this planet has both strengths and weaknesses. One's strength may be the ability to draw so well that the picture looks like real life, but their weakness lies in the ability to do math. Everybody's strengths and weaknesses differ from each other, so it is a time waster to compare yourself with others. Instead, use that time to improve on whatever it is you need to help you climb to new heights.

Dwelling on the things you aren't good at to the point that you defeat yourself from trying anything won't help you achieve your goals. Looking at yourself with the mindset to identify areas to work on in order to achieve your goals will make all the difference in the end. You don't have to become great at everything, but if something is holding you back from where you want to go, then it's time to get real with yourself.

It is tough looking at yourself and coming up with negative or downgrading realities that reflect your current state. This has been a challenge since humans first existed. Everybody wants to be perfect.

No one wants any problems in their life. Who doesn't want that "make money and relax" kind of life?

The average person doesn't want anybody telling them sad truths about themselves. They instead want comfort and for everybody to be on their team. When they see a problem, they run and do their best to avoid it.

Self-assessing is not fun. Oh hell, it can be not just difficult, but it can hurt. It can make you feel like ripping yourself apart. That's something you may want to run from on occasion. But lying to yourself is ten times worse.

What I mean by lying to yourself is you think, *I'm perfect, and absolutely nothing in my life needs improvement.* You may deep down know that there is something you need to improve on to become a better person, but you choose not to admit it, because facing it will hurt your feelings.

What that means is that you will not come to terms with yourself about needing to improve something, because you are afraid of feeling like you're not good enough. You want to be perfect.

It's all about the looks—and not the process. You're afraid of feeling that pain. You want to be good at whatever it is—overnight. You avoid that realization that you need to improve and that you are NOT perfect.

Sorry champ, but that avoidance tactic that comes out just because something is hard or hurts doesn't work today. We all have our strengths and weaknesses, and to develop those strengths you have to work on those weaknesses. It's common sense. Why do you think we have all of this technology today? People like Steve Jobs, Bill Gates, Mark Zuckerberg, etc., had that drive to become the cream of the crop. Do you really think that if they had lied to themselves, saying for example that they could make or contribute to the finest piece of technology overnight, that we would have their inventions today?

They knew their innovations would take time. In fact, they knew it would take years and years to make their mark. If Steve Jobs (1955-2011) said, "By tomorrow, the iPhone will be a bestseller," back in 2007 when the first iPhone came out, he would've put no effort into his invention or marketing because he would've been more than certain that his product would be a success. He would have become cocky with himself and said, "I'm done. That's all the work that needs to be done."

To be clear, that is never the case—nothing huge and life-changing comes overnight. A success story does not ever start with, "Last night, I went to sleep as a nobody and woke up to find myself in the hall of fame." The biggest accomplishments always start with a story of a dream, a passion, and the rollercoaster of events that led the successful person to become who they are today.

So why would Jobs lie to himself, saying that he didn't have to do any work, that his product would become the most fantastic on the market in less than twelve hours? In fact, over the years, he continued to improve upon the product as he heard from users about what worked and didn't—and as technology and customers' needs changed. For example, he tried to release the Apple Lisa, the Apple company's first computer, in 1983.

It seemed like a great idea, but it failed to become popular in the market. The high price, alongside its malfunctions, made it near impossible for Jobs to sell.

He took this failure and didn't let it deter him from becoming one of the most successful men in the world. If he had lied to himself and shortcut that process, we wouldn't have the iPhone. It would have failed before it became a household name.

Imagine that. For some of you reading this, can you imagine yourself without Candy Crush or Subway Surfers or Tik Tok?

Lying overall is just a bad thing to do. Whether you lie to your friend or a family member or a coach, it isn't right. The truth will always be waiting for you. There's a quote from the late, iconic, American-born singer Elvis Presley that states, "Truth is like the sun. You can shut it out for a time, but it ain't going away." The truth is there to stay forever. Every lie will soon be unfolded, and the truth will come out and show off.

If you want to achieve a certain goal, know that the road won't be easy. While you are driving on that road, don't tell yourself that the car (or your life) will drive itself, and no work will be necessary. That mentality will get you nowhere.

If you know you need to work on something and know deep down that the job needs to be done, do the job. Telling yourself, "Well, I do really know that I need to work on it, but it takes up too much of my time," will not only ruin the whole mentality and incentive of the Hunger for Improvement, which is to continually grow, but it will get you nowhere.

If the thought of achieving something great or making a small improvement even pops into your mind for a split second, there's a reason why you thought of it. It didn't come for no reason. You *do* need to work on something.

And if you choose to go through life like that, avoiding the work, the only place you'll ever be is the starting line. But your starting line won't actually be considered the "start." It will be called the finish line, because you won't be willing to do what it takes to improve. Basically, you will have already quit–by not escalating your life to the next level.

The truth is always stronger than a lie, and that's just factual. So next time you want to lie, you will be safe only temporarily. Just like lying to yourself about your current level of development, it may seem comforting at first to tell a lie to others. But you will get hurt in the long run.

Be real to yourself, and don't hide anything that you know you need to work on. You know deep down inside that you need to work on it, and if you lay off your focus on the areas you need to improve, you will feel worse from the guilt trip it brings. Swallow the pill of what you need to work on, and do it—for example, running a mile in under seven minutes or becoming the president of the company at which you work.

You want to reach that level, right? Lying will have you backpedaling instead of front pedaling. Your life will go in reverse.

I will give you a real-life example of when I lied to myself and instantly regretted it.

There have been times when I would say to myself, "Okay, I know this, yada yada yada," while studying, because I was either tired in general, tired of studying, or indeed distracted by something not related to studying. To be brutally honest, I am sure we have all been here. I would just leave my study session or go on to study something else.

A few of those times, however, I did not know the material, even though I said to myself I did. I lied to myself. I told myself that I knew the material, so I would feel accomplished.

I would be fine the night before the exam, but once I was handed the test, I automatically regretted lying to myself. I paid the price, which was getting the answers wrong.

Which dropped my grade in that class. Which potentially dropped my GPA a bit. Which just led to more pressure to keep my GPA up.

Lying literally creates a domino effect, as you can see from my example. You lie to yourself, which can lead to something sort of little, but that can affect something else, and so on.

Even worse, lying to yourself can make you feel good temporarily, and who doesn't want that good feeling? You may develop a habit of lying to yourself to feel good and get out of putting in the work. This can lead to an unprecedented comfort zone, which is a topic I will talk about very shortly.

You can go from finish to start at any time in your life. You just need to apply yourself—and take time out of your day to focus on what is needed to elevate yourself.

Besides complacency, causing you to remain on the starting line, other factors can derail you. One major derailer in implementing a Hunger to Improve is your desire to avoid fear. If you're too scared to come to reality with yourself, because you don't want to hurt your own feelings, that's your comfort zone driving you. The comfort zone is a no-no—a wasteland where nothing great will be produced. Your comfort zone is the place where you stay to avoid every problem or anything that bothers you. That comfort zone drives away any fear and keeps you isolated from life.

Sounds good at first, right? No fear, no problems. Things that make you happy are all around you. Your safety is mighty strong. No worries, everything is good.

Well the comfort zone may seem like an option, if you are willing to stay the same or downgrade. But you need new experiences to get through life. You cannot gain experience from sitting at your house, doing nothing or something mindless, and avoiding interaction. For example, watching Netflix all day or sleeping all day can actually drain you of your life skills, and when it's time to step outside of your front door and interact with reality, you won't know where to begin.

Seems like a situation you do not wish to put yourself into, right? Your comfort zone is toxic to your goals. It is poison. Try your best not to make it your closest friend. Step outside of your comfort zone, and take on your life in full swing. It's your life, so why not make the best of it? Why not see what life has to offer?

Your comfort zone is mostly a peace of mind. It's not an actual place, unless you consider a certain facility or area on Earth your comfort zone. So since your mind makes this comfort zone up, and it's not tangible, what is stopping you from escaping something that really isn't there?

When I would get my exam back after not studying enough, I always found my head in between my hands in repentance. I knew that if I would've studied even five minutes more, I would have increased my chance of getting the questions right. My ego and regret bit me in the butt.

Do not lie to yourself. Do that extra rep, or study for those extra five minutes, if you're still uncertain.

Uncertainty is usually a sign that you are not fluent. Be honest with yourself about how prepared you are for the next step. Dishonesty brings a costly price.

Self-Reflection Rest Stop

Welcome back! Time to do some more self-reflection! Time to potentially become a better you!

1. When was the last time you self-assessed yourself? Did it do you any good?

2. How many times have you lied to yourself? Which was the worst time? What price did you pay?

3. What did you learn from that experience of lying to yourself? Do you try to avoid lying to yourself due to the lesson you learned?

4. What exists in your comfort zone? Have you ever avoided doing something outside of your comfort zone? What was it?

5. Have you learned the hard way yet about the comfort zone? If not, is what I am telling you giving you an incentive to avoid learning the hard way about the comfort zone?

Chapter 4

My Heart is What Keeps Me Going

Every human and every animal on this planet, ever since the dawn of time, has had a heart. Without your heart, nutrients and oxygen wouldn't flow throughout your body to keep you standing and performing daily functions. And without your heart beating, you're equivalent to dead. Your heart is part of your cardiovascular system, which plays a big role in keeping you alive and well.

Your body has eleven different major body systems, and without one working, it can cause a domino effect. This means that your body will stop working insidiously.

So to keep your heart going, you have probably learned to eat right, exercise, get good amounts of rest, etc. Your heart is what keeps you in motion and caught up with your life. If you didn't have a heart, you wouldn't be reading this right now.

Your heart does more than keep you physically alive, however. It also gives you a reason for living—through the emotions of the heart.

I bet that you love at least one person or thing, no matter who or what it is. When you have that love, you want to be surrounded by it and make sure it lasts forever. You can't—or don't want to—imagine yourself without that love.

You know you have that love for something when it overloads your heart, and you want to do everything you can to keep that love active and alive.

Transfer that to your passion now.

Going back to the football analogy, ever since you developed that passion for football, your dream of getting to that next level invades your mind, and all you want to do is improve. That passion is backed by love. Love is the deeper value that drives the passion.

Without loving an activity, it is difficult to want to do it and become the best version of yourself you can possibly be. So before you really want to take off with something, think if you really love whatever it is you're doing—and if the passion can remain permanent to allow you to pursue excellence with that dream.

This is a way to tell if you really love something or not. When you love someone, often you can't stop thinking of them, right? They infiltrate your mind, and all you want to do is be with that significant other. Every time you are separated from that person, you may feel lonely or sad.

Now apply that concept to your so called "passion." Does it take over your mind? Are there periods of time when you cannot stop thinking about it? Do you metaphorically want to "marry it"? If the answer is yes to one or more of these questions, I think it is safe to say that you love whatever it is you're doing.

With love comes disappointment. Be aware of that. People often experience this conflict or sense of loss. You fall in love with somebody, and you may have the time of your lives together. But in a relationship, there will be arguments, fights, etc. That love will be tested. Now there's a way of testing if the love surrounding the two people is strong. They could have the biggest fight and not talk to each other for days, or maybe even weeks. But if that love is phenomenal and the strongest ever, the two will find a way to work things out, no matter how long it takes.

On the other hand, let's say another two people in a relationship— Jessica and Jason—get into a fight and don't talk for the same amount of time. If both people continue not to talk to each other and never reach out, even if Jessica knows that she was wrong but doesn't wish to admit it, the relationship won't thrive. Jessica obviously doesn't care about the strength of the relationship as much as being right. All she cares about may be not looking guilty or staying in a position where she can still fight back. This relationship becomes more about who has control, rather than about sharing love. Jessica knows that this ongoing distance and stubbornness indeed will ruin the relationship—but only cares about looks and herself.

This pattern of behavior says that the relationship is not strong. Or the love may exist with Jason, but not with Jessica.

In order for a strong relationship to stay intact, love has to remain no matter what happens. Love must be expressed from both of the lovers. And in this situation, it is pretty obvious that the love isn't reciprocated between the two. After one fall, one struggle or argument, it's game over.

Now enough with the relationship talk. Let's put these terms into the context of someone who is trying to achieve something great. Like I've stated, love will be tested and is disappointing at times. Love works the same way when you are investing your passion in your dream. Say, for example, you try out for an elite football team. You give it your all, but you do not make it onto the roster.

Now this is where your love for that dream is tested. You are undoubtedly very disappointed that you didn't make the team. However, this is where you have a choice between one of two outcomes. One outcome is you can give up and say that your love for football is ruined due to this event, and you will never return to football, because of the amount of distraught emotions your failure gave you. OR, you can take this failure as a learning lesson, and keep moving forward.

Let's explore how this plays out. Imagine that David is the one who quit playing football, and Jake is the one who kept moving forward. If David had experienced just one fall and quit, it is pretty easy to see that he doesn't abide by the fact that success comes with hardship. If the love were strong, David would've refused to give up and wanted to work even harder. He would've known that nothing worth having comes easy.

On the other hand, Jake has such a strong love for football that failure is just a lesson that will not stand in the way of the climb. Jake won't give up on his love, because he refuses to let one downfall become a final destination. He will do whatever it takes to protect that love and persist. He indeed knows that nothing worth having comes easy.

Times of trouble have always ignited an even bigger flame in me. When I would fail in something that I cared deeply about, I wouldn't stop until I fixed whatever it was that I failed at.

For example, when I first started learning how to take slap shots in hockey, they were mighty difficult at first to even understand. A slap shot is the hardest shot in hockey. It's when you bring your hockey stick up into the air and hit the puck as hard as you can. Success of a slap shot looks like the puck goes towards the net in a straight line at a fast and steady pace, with no wavering or wobbling. A failure of a slap shot looks like the puck is wobbling towards the net and going at a slow and unsteady pace.

Instead of complaining about how hard slapshots were, I worked at them to nauseum. My love for hockey was enormous, and I couldn't give up on that love. It took me months to get the technique right. I worked at it every day, and even before practice, I started working on them in my own little corner.

Guess what? Now I know how to take a slap shot—all thanks to my heart and my desire to not quit.

Side note: let me tell you, it felt amazing when I got that slapshot down. To think that I was on the brink of giving up because it wasn't coming naturally to me for a long while—that turned into even more fire to get better at it, and eventually led me to knowing how to fluently take a slapshot. I remember I was in practice for my travel team, I did the slapshot, and I froze. I was like, "Is this real life right now?" I yelled, "YES, BABY! LET'S GO!" and other sentences in excitement, and threw a few fist pumps into the air. My teammates looked at me like I was crazy. They didn't understand what had just happened, so I let it slide. It felt so good, and I had the biggest smile on my face under my cage and mouthguard.

The moment that I finally got the slapshot and celebrated made me realize even more that nothing could stop me from the sport I loved. That success declared that my love for hockey was stronger than my weariness. That declared that my heart truly did keep me going—even with the major difficulty that I faced.

Doesn't that sound like an experience that you would want to have, even if it's once in your life? Where you finally overcome an obstacle and can give credit to how huge your love is for whatever it is you're doing?

So, the bottom line is, your heart is what keeps you going, both literally and metaphorically. You need your heart to pump and stay active in order to perform daily life functions and activities—and stay alive. Metaphorically, your heart is what keeps you going in times of trouble and keeps your passion alive. Without a heart you wouldn't be alive— and you wouldn't love. Therefore, there's no passion without your heart—nothing to really look forward to.

Everybody on this planet has a heart. The outcome all depends on who actually uses it and who doesn't. Everybody has the capability of loving someone or something—that is something we have in common. However, it takes time, just like everything in life.

You have a heart for your whole life, so why not use it? It is very much capable of extraordinary things!

Self-Reflection Rest Stop

Welcome back! Time to do some more self-reflection! Time to potentially become a better you!

1. Who is someone that you love? What is something that you love?

2. Would you do anything to keep that relationship alive with that person whom you love? How about with that thing that you love?

3. Have you ever gotten into a fight or gone through a dark time with those loves? What was the result? Why do you think the results came out the way that they did?

4. When you were wrong in a situation, did you choose to fix it or think you could not give in? Do you regret your decision, whatever that decision may be? Was the result that you really had the love—or you really didn't have it?

5. If you experienced something spectacular after almost giving up on a love of yours, how did it feel?

Chapter 5

Be Patient with The Results

Before anybody starts a new goal, they automatically think of the potential results. They have their minds set on the future they can possibly seize. They think of what they want to happen. They have their eyes on the prize. I mean, if there were no prizes to reward at the end, then a lot of us would not work hard—or would give up.

Whether you will get to your goal truly depends on your mentality. For a minute or so, think to yourself. With no lying, ask yourself this question: do you care more about the reward, or do you care more about the self-progress you make while trying to get that reward? Which means more to you?

Unlike many other questions given to you on a daily basis, whether in school or somewhere else, there's no right or wrong answer. Your answer is self-proclaimed, individual. Your mind is yours. Whatever choice you make for what you think is more important, your feelings are valid. Your thoughts are what make you, *you*. This is the no-judge zone.

40

Now I'm going to get real with you. There has probably been a time in your life, or more than one time, when you were doing everything you could to get to the next level— to where you wanted to be. But you got frustrated, because you weren't there yet. You got discouraged, because you weren't moving up the ladder as quickly as you thought you should be. You were hard on yourself, and at one point, you probably either wanted to give up, almost gave up, or did give up. You thought to yourself, *I'm putting in all this work, day by day, doing what others won't do, but find myself not moving up.* You feel that you are staying in the same place. Almost like you keep digging, and there isn't any value as far as the eye can see. Maybe you see others moving up the ladder more quickly than you, and you get discouraged. You think, *Why not me? Why them? What did they do to deserve this?* And maybe the people who are moving up the ladder more rapidly than you don't put in half of the amount work you do! That's frustrating, isn't it?

I have been in this situation countless times. You know, I would be working constantly to improve myself in whatever it is, and I would see others getting rewarded for what I believed I should get rewarded for. This happened a lot in hockey—and with trying to maintain fitness. Amongst other things, like math class. I would workout and practice hockey constantly, alongside practice math, and people who did not do half of what I did to improve themselves got the results quicker—and they were the ones who got noticed by others.

This would frustrate the absolute hell out of me. This mentality didn't just break me and make me feel even worse, it also took control of my mind. I couldn't stop thinking, *I won't get anywhere, ever. I can't make it to the top, because of other people's success. I should just quit, because it's no use. I'm not moving; others are. I'm not getting rewarded; others are.*

I'm working my tail off and not seeing the results; others aren't working even half as hard as I am, and they're seeing results.

On the contrary, do you want to know something that begins with T and ends in E? That's been around since the world began? The thing that we live within and that we observe on our watches and phones and wall clocks? The word is TIME.

Time is needed for everything. Time is needed if you want to develop. Think of it this way: at one point, you were a baby. You couldn't speak, only scream or laugh or cry. You couldn't walk, only crawl. You couldn't do anything you can do today. Now look at you. You have mastered daily life skills and use them without even realizing it. Reading this right now is something you couldn't do as a baby! Do you know why you can do all of this? Besides passion to get better (your Hunger for Improvement), you had one important tool working for you: time.

Time lends itself for you to develop. Time lends itself for you to progress. Without time, you would still be a baby who couldn't control anything. Maybe you wouldn't even be born! Because of time, you are grown up and can take control of your own life and make decisions for yourself. Time has developed you from a baby to your age now, and will continue to develop you 'til the day you die. You used time to work on what you needed to progress in, right? Time is on your side.

Now that we are in the topic of time, let's discuss how time may be different between one person and another. Let's just say you are standing next to someone who can write in script, but you can't just yet. You both are in the same class, learning at the same time, and the same thing. The person next to you just gets a better handle of writing in script than you—at first. You take more time to get a handle of it, like you write more slowly and steadily. You keep practicing and practicing, and eventually one day you can write just like the person that was next to you, maybe even better. You're very happy and pleased with yourself that you accomplished this feat, but wonder why that person who was standing next to you mastered it faster.

I'll give you the answer right now. Are you ready? The answer is to not compare yourself with someone else's success. Comparisons don't work. Everybody on this planet has different abilities and weaknesses. Comparing yourself to someone else is a complete waste of time and a great self-destructing mechanism. If you want to self-destruct yourself, by all means compare yourself to others. But who in their right mind wants to destroy themselves?

Now that you hopefully understand that comparing yourself to others is a horrible thing to do, let's focus on you and your growth timeline. Let's just say today you think of a goal that you wish to accomplish. And today you start to work to achieve that goal. A week goes by—no, two weeks go by—and you find yourself either improving mighty insidiously or not improving at all. Something you must remember is the minute you put the food in the microwave is not the minute you eat the food. The hour you put the turkey for Thanksgiving dinner in the oven is not the hour you eat it.

The beginning is always the hardest, as I said before. BEGINning. Begin, the start, the first step, the first stride. You need a beginning in order to escalate. It's impossible for you to get the results on the first day or the first couple of days.

Without a beginning, where would you be? Every successful person in this world was once a beginner. You need a platform from which to elevate.

If you keep pushing and keep striving, it will come. You have to let time do its thing. Time works for YOU! No matter how long it may take you to accomplish whatever it is you wish to do, time will do what is best for you. Patience is key when wanting things. The longer you wait, the sweeter it is when you receive it. The harder you work, the more amazing it is to finally reach your goal. The results will come. Just keep pushing, and be patient.

The day when those results appear in your hands will feel amazing, if you keep going! Time is on your side; always remember that. Unless you're running late for soccer practice, then that's a different story!

If you have trouble remembering the importance of letting time work for you, remember this: the minute that you put the popcorn in the microwave is not the minute you eat it. It's just kernels.

Self-Reflection Rest Stop

Welcome back! Time for some more self-reflection! Time to potentially become a better you!

1. In which areas of your life do you struggle the most with maintaining patience?

2. Does the feeling of impatience drive your will to become better or set it back?

3. Realistically, how long do you think it will take to reach your current goal? Are you willing to accept that amount of time and practice patience?

4. Do you often compare yourself with others? Do you think you can try to put an end to it? If so, how?

5. What do you believe is the most unique about yourself? Do you compare that with others?

Chapter 6

The View will Look Beautiful

When you live in an apartment on a high level of a building, most likely you will get a great view. You are located multiple stories high and can see everything that goes on inferior to you, on the ground. You can see people walking around, cars pulling in and out, and if you're lucky enough, maybe a view of a beautiful city.

Or in another scenario, maybe you take a trip to a place like New Hampshire (in my case) and decide to drive up Mt. Washington. You feel excitement build as you're driving up the mountain, because you know that the climb will be worth it. Once you reach the top, you get out of your car and observe something that a lot of people in this world may never get a chance to see: the gorgeous scenery of the white mountains—and if you're in the right place at the right time, maybe even a marvelous sunrise or sunset view. Who wouldn't want that? I'm sure that some time in your life you have hiked or driven somewhere and taken a step back to see the beautiful view waiting for you as you approached it (or drove up the mountain).

I've always been a fan of settings like this that make me feel a sense of awe. One summer, my family and I drove up Prospect Mountain located in Lake George, New York. It took a while to ascend it because of how windy and narrow the roads were, but when we reached the top, it was so worth it. We saw the gorgeous Green Mountains of Vermont in the near distance—and the whole town of Lake George (which, by the way, if you ask me, is an excellent vacation spot).

I recommend you take a trip up. How did we get the opportunity to see the amazing view? We moved up the mountain. If we would've stayed on the ground, we wouldn't have seen anything from a bird's eye view. In seeing the town from a normal human standpoint, something that us humans are exposed to every day, we would not have challenged or inspired ourselves with a new perspective.

So now let's put this concept into metaphorical terms. The only reason why I could see the gorgeous view at Prospect Mountain is because I went up the mountain. My family and I drove halfway up the mountain and then walked the other half just because it was a beautiful day out. The only way that you can or will ever be able to see such a view is by climbing and working. This is literally how life works. You only can see the progress you've made if you work to get to another vantage point. Progress doesn't come from sitting down and watching television. Your knowledge on certain characters in a certain television show may increase, but will that help you with making a living or developing essential life skills?

No sweetie, I don't think so. There's nothing wrong with watching television, but instead of watching it eight hours a day, cut it down to four, so you can spend the other four hours doing something that you will be proud of yourself for—or even thirty minutes to an hour to start. It's always good to do something that will make you feel at peace within yourself when you lay your head down on the pillow at night. That sense of satisfaction is one of the best feelings. It starts with baby steps. Do one good and/or educational thing each day, and I'm telling you, in the days to come, you'll find yourself as a different person. Or should I say, upgraded.

Now this may sound bizarre, but you don't necessarily need to reach the absolute top in order to see a nice view. While you're climbing and working up the hill, you can look and see the progress you've made. You can be halfway and still see a gorgeous view. Every step equals a better overlook. So if you feel as if you're not where you want to be just yet, this does not in any way mean that you can't see a view that is worthwhile and inspiring. Your work to get up that mountain is the key in the process, and self-evaluation allows you to look over your progress and improve along the way. Your work is what gets you to see that view. Don't hesitate to look around, even if you're not at the top yet. It's better to have peripheral vision, where you can see everything around you, than tunnel vision, where all you see are more steps that don't end for a while.

Tunnel vision is preached as an ideal by many people on this planet. The definition of tunnel vision is the tendency to focus excessively on a goal with no distractions. In a way, this is a good thing to have. But what's included with tunnel vision is looking only ahead, with an inability to look to your left or right. Maybe there's a nice view on the side of your path, but you can't see it because you're in a tunnel. I'm not saying that tunnel vision is an absolutely terrible thing. I'm saying that it's not ideal to have it 24/7, because you will in fact miss out on the opportunity to see the progress you've made. You will in fact also miss out on the opportunities you could encounter and possibly take on during the process— opportunities that could be life-long beneficial or elevate you even higher.

Tunnel vision focuses on the climb. There's no way, or it is prohibited, to look around—so that "no distractions" are encountered. Yet it's self-rewarding to look at the progress you've made, rather than just keep focusing on the ground you haven't covered just yet. Just think of the quote from the movie *Ferris Bueller's Day Off*: "Life moves pretty fast. If you don't stop and look around once in a while, you could miss it." It's a comical movie, but this quote nails it right in the brain.

I am a big believer in being impeccable with yourself. This means that you are true to yourself, and you know what you are capable of and not capable of. The opportunity to have peripheral vision can show you all the progress you have made. That proves that you can do whatever you want, at your own pace. You know what your morals are. You know how fast or slow you wish to climb up the mountain. You know which views you can and want to see at certain times. As long as you're improving, that's all that matters.

You are in control of yourself. Always remember that! It may seem like you are "out of control" at times, but there's no one living inside of you. You are you. Your destiny and your improvement are completely in your hands.

So overall, the view gets better as you climb. It's way cooler to see the world at a bird's eye view than at a human's eye view, on the ground. So next time you go on a hike with your friends or family and stop at a point to set up a picnic to relax, eat, and look at the view, know that this goes for your goals too.

Or even if you're going to the top floor of a building, think of this concept too. Even if you live around flat land, go to a wide, open farm area and look around.

Look at the distance you can travel if you put in the work. You'll be able to see another distance that your eye couldn't pick up on at the start.

The top is something that we all want to reach, but it takes time to get there. And the ONLY way to get there is to climb. There's no magic elevator that will get you there. If you thought there was, sorry to burst your bubble. Actually no, I'm not sorry, because I don't want you having that mentality. Your work is what gets you to climb, which gets you to see a view, which means that you're closer to your goal than you were when you started. Amazing things and views lie within the climb—and of course, after the climb. Keep going; don't you want to see those beautiful views?!

Self-Reflection Rest Stop

Welcome back! Time to do some more self-reflection! Time to potentially become a better you!

1. How many times have you climbed or gone up an elevation to see a nice view? Did this view put the question of how and why you got up there into your mind?

2. When trying to reach a goal, do you prefer not to stop and self-evaluate until you reach the goal, or do you prefer to take some time for self-evaluation and give yourself credit on the way to your goal? Have you ever changed your mind?

3. Has that decision of how you choose to climb (going off of question 2) impacted you in a positive or negative way? Do you think your process has affected the speed of reaching that goal?

4. Have you heard of the phrase "tunnel vision" many times? Who or what tried to instill it into your head? How did you like it? Do you think it did you more bad than good, or vice versa?

5. Have you ever tried to use your peripheral vision? If not, do you plan on it?

Chapter 7

The Puzzle Fits Perfectly

I don't know if it is recognizable to you, but I put the chapters in alignment with how the process of the Hunger for Improvement works progressively. You understand what it means, then you develop it by finding something that you can't go a day without thinking about. That hunger leads you to focus on getting to your destination.

In addition, never forget that lying is not a good thing to do; it goes against the whole HFI concept. Your heart is what keeps you alive, literally. Your heart is what keeps you going in real life, encountering whatever it is you face. And with everything that is explained in this book, *reality* can be linked to *mentality*. What you do in real life can transform into an actual thought process that sticks with you to achieve what you once thought was impossible.

You know how they say, "Good things come to those who wait"? Well it's true. Patience is key when trying to achieve something. Comparing yourself to others just rushes the process for you, but it's only rushed in your head. It's poison to compare yourself to others, because it disrupts you from your abilities and just serves to make you feel bad about yourself. What is in your head is not in reality.

In addition, to rush a process that needs time to develop will only defeat you. Be patient with the results. The minute you put the frozen chicken nuggets in the oven is not the minute you eat them. See, another *reality to mentality* reference!

To reiterate, those results can only be attained by climbing. The climb gives you results which are like views. The view that I saw when I went up Prospect Mountain can translate to my progress in what I'm trying to achieve.

That goes for you too. Views only come from climbs, and if you're not at the top yet, don't hesitate to look around and see the progress you've made. Looking at yourself compared to where you were at the beginning can only serve to encourage you. Confidence comes out of this perspective of looking over how far you've come. Confidence is an amazing feeling, which leads to endless opportunities.

To be clear, it is also important to know and understand how to grip that confidence and keep it tamed, if it turns your ego all the way up. Too much confidence is not good at times, especially when you're trying to reach a goal, because you may stop working hard and pledge to yourself that you're better than the world. You tell yourself that you're king of the hill, cream of the crop, big fish in a small pond, etc. Once you lose your ego, you will find that you made a fool of yourself. An absolute fool.

A perfect example of when this happened to me when a couple of times in high school, I understood a topic so easily that I didn't think I needed to study that much. I always studied for each quiz and test, because I wanted to get the highest grade possible. But at times my confidence would get too high, and it would lead me to skim over the notes once, say "I'm done," shut my notebook, and go do something that I actually wanted to do.

Once in chemistry class, sophomore year of high school, I thought I knew a topic so well that I barely studied for the exam. I only maybe looked over a few questions. I honestly don't remember the topic since it was quite a while ago. I do remember the wave of guilt I felt when my teacher handed me my test with the back side of the exam facing up rather than the front. I don't know what it is like at the schools you attended, but all throughout my school years thus far, when a teacher handed back an exam with the back facing up, you already knew you didn't do so hot. Literally so many times when I would get my exams handed back to me, I would pray that the paper was laid down with the front side facing upwards.

Everyone in my classes felt the same way. We would all look at each other with either a smirk on our faces—or our lips clenched together and our eyes wide open.

Going back to my exam being handed back to me, the exam was back-side up, so I already knew that I would not be too pleased with my score. I believe my score was around a 60, to the extent that I can remember. I looked at my classmate who sat across from me and clenched my lips together. She gave me the "what did you get?" look. You probably know that look, when the person's eyebrows are down to their eyes in curiosity and they may tilt their head. I hesitated at first, but I showed her my score, and she made a "ssss" sound. Not referring to a snake, but a sound that exclaims the words, "Oh dang, that's not good my friend."

I bit my tongue and automatically stared at the table. I remember walking out of class, ashamed of myself, realizing that my confidence got too much of me. This was a learning lesson for me, as I knew that I had to put in the extra work, no matter how confident I was. Obviously, according to the exam, I didn't know the material as well as I thought I did.

Boy, was that a "honey, you would've thought" moment. A slap in the face.

Too much of anything is no good. Just like too much candy can make you feel sick or lead to an unhealthy lifestyle, too much healthy food like broccoli can lead to an upset stomach because of its high amounts of fiber. Broccoli is good for you, but too much of anything is not good. Balance is key. Too much confidence, even though it may seem amazing at first, can turn to the worst for you, if you don't put it on a leash. Too much insecurity about yourself can lead to staying inside a bubble and not getting out and exploring opportunities, because you don't feel as if you can do it.

Believing in yourself is a huge priority and a first step when you want to achieve something. I really cannot express how important it is to believe in yourself. It's literally a magic potion to make you confident in using your abilities to help you go far. If you don't believe in yourself, you won't put the work in, simply because you will feel as if you can't accomplish it. When you don't put in the work, it shows, because you're not improving. When you're not improving, others around you can wonder what's going on and unfortunately lose their confidence in you. Who will believe in you, if you don't believe in yourself?

It is also very important not to care about what everyone else thinks of you. Sometimes you do need those critics and supporters to help you get to where you want to be. You need the critics to tell you what you need to work on in order to expand your knowledge to improve, and you need the supporters to help you get through the tough times and give you positivity when no one else will. Both are vital to one's development, not just in a certain sport or career, but in life overall. They can be a huge help if you're in the position where you're lying to yourself. Deep down you may know that you're not being truthful to yourself, but one thing to remember is that others around you, especially those who know you very well, can have a sixth sense of detecting your deceptive behavior. An imbalance to either extreme—enabling you in the wrong behavior or criticizing you when you are doing your best—is no good.

Surround yourself with those who will assist you in the climb, both *incline critics* and supporters. What I mean by incline critics are those who criticize you for the sake of your development. They don't criticize you because they want to see you fail, they criticize because they want to let you know what you need to work on, and in addition, they will give you tools on how to fix whatever it is you need to work on. I came up with this term just recently, actually. Don't surround yourself with those critics who just want to see you fail all the time. Don't give energy to the ones who want to see you lose. Those types of critics can feed fuel to the fire of passion burning in your heart, but they can also get into your head for deterioration if you let them. These are the types that you want to try to not give a damn about what they think, because it doesn't matter. Incline critics are the real deal.

Believing in yourself will lead you to work hard, which will draw in supporters and critics, because you're improving. And that improvement becomes your fuel for life itself.

The Hunger for Improvement is essential when it comes to achieving a goal, or more importantly, going through life. Hunger isn't satisfied until something that is wanted, or should I say needed in many circumstances, is received. It is 100 percent possible for you to tap into and feed this hunger. And that's a promise. Anybody can develop this hunger; it just depends on who is more hungry for improvement and who is willing to bring it on.

Remember, it can last from days to weeks to months to years, maybe even a lifetime, depending on how huge the hunger is and how long it lasts. Depending on what goal you have, if the desire to improve in any aspect of life is inhabited inside oneself, the Everlasting Hunger to Improve will become your vital driving force.

I bleed the HFI. It is in my veins. Do you?

Self-Reflection Rest Stop

Welcome back! Time for some more self-reflection! Time to potentially become a better you!

1. Have you ever had an experience like I did when your ego bit you in the butt? What happened? Did it teach you a lesson?

2. What was the longest improvement process that you've ever endured? Was it worth the patience?

3. Do you let what people say about you, or to you, get to your heart too easily? Or do you shrug it off?

4. How do you take compliments and criticism? Do you accept both—or only accept one of them?

5. Do you have trouble believing in yourself? If so, does this prevent you from trying to achieve? What do you think you could do to switch that mentality?

Conclusion: The Finish Line

**Whistle blows, horns go off,
crowd goes crazy rah rah rah*!*

I want to take this time to say that I honestly hope that I inspired you with this book. Thank you for reading. No matter what position you may find yourself in now, whether a good one or bad one, I hope you take heed of what I said and use the Hunger for Improvement principles for all life situations that apply.

You have a 100 percent chance of becoming the best version of yourself that you always wanted to be. Tell that to yourself every day, because one day you will reach that 100 percent due to convincing yourself that your goal was possible.

Whatever you repeat becomes a habit. And I really think that the repetition of giving yourself the benefit of the doubt, showering yourself with positive thoughts about your potential, can have a humongous impact on you—in a good way.

Once you have reached this habit of thought, you have reached a whole new and improved level of freedom.

"The Hunger for Improvement never ends."

—Me

Bonus Side Note:
How Can You Get Involved
with Your Community?

I want to add this, to expand on the discussion of helping others. It may have sounded interesting, what is explained on the back of this book. You may have even filed it in your mind as something to think about. But let me tell you, that you can do the same thing. It just takes the courage and will to want to help.

It plays into the process of *developing a passion* for helping others. You have a heart. Are you finding something to apply it to? This is a great start.

Do not be afraid to reach out to clubs or organizations. They're always looking for people to get involved. All it takes is a phone call or an email.

If you are not a fan of clubs or crowds, do not worry. You don't have to be involved in something formal to help your community. Literally, you can start by just picking up a piece of trash off the street. Start by performing one act of kindness per day—for example holding the door open for someone, or if someone drops something, picking it up for them. You don't have to do everything for recognition. In fact, *doing things in the dark shows integrity.*

Eventually, doing acts like this every day will increase your incentive to want to do them even more. Seeing others smile because of you is an incredible feeling, isn't it? You may want to see more people smile because of you, and this can make you want to do more. It's a process—and you will see progress!

Even smiling to someone on the street is exceptional. They could be having a bad day, and you smiling at them can brighten their spirits.

Smiles are contagious! So is laughter! If you know me well, you know I love to do both to a great extent!

For years, I have been committed to hard work and putting others before myself. If someone next to me needed help, I would make sure they got what they needed before I had my needs met. And I still do to this day. I get self-satisfaction when I see someone smiling because of me or see someone's day get better because of me.

One example of an experience I had helping in my community actually changed my career goals, from wanting to major in athletic training to switching to occupational therapy (OT). Yes, for a good portion of my life I actually wanted to go into Athletic training. In the summer of 2019, I volunteered as a mentor at a program on Long Island called Inclusive Sports and Fitness, or ISF for short. It is a program that works with special needs kids on their motor skills and overall life skills they need to have daily. I volunteered alongside professional occupational therapists (OTs), and their work astonished me.

Occupational Therapy, for those who don't know, is the branch of health care that assists physical, sensory, and motor skills in people who need the help. That's exactly what I did at ISF.

The OTs made the kids feel so happy. The kids would go home that day better at a specific skill. Just seeing how the OTs worked with the kids, how nice the OTs were to me, and how they taught me how to work with the kids really made me want to become an OT too.

I even did OT work under the supervision of the professionals, and I fell in love with it. I loved working with the kids and assisting them. Seeing them smile, laugh, and have a good time was literally a gift—so rewarding. We made learning fun for them, and they were exposed to new exercises that they enjoyed.

This experience I had that summer was life-changing for me, and I can confidently say that in a good way. It all started because I got involved in helping my community.

What can you do to get involved and help someone? What will you to today to act on that Hunger for Improvement in your community?

About The Author

My name is Jordan Salzano, and I am from Long Island, New York. I grew up with my mom and dad, my younger sister, and my nana and papa. As of the publishing of this book, I recently graduated from the Hoosac School, a co-educational prep and boarding school. I am attending Springfield College, which is located in Springfield, Massachusetts. I am studying both Occupational Therapy and Communications, and I aspire to get degrees in both fields.

I also aspire to become a powerful motivational speaker who influences people from all over the world. That is something I am so hungry for. It is a dream that never escapes my mind.

In fact, you could say that speaking and motivating others is an *enormous passion* of mine.

I want to inspire others who have gone through what I have, to motivate students and others to always remember the Hunger for Improvement points that I bring up in this book. (More points and books to come, by the way. This is only the beginning of my journey, and I am beyond excited to share this with you all!)

Feel free to follow and direct message me with any feedback, or if you have any questions! I am always willing to talk!

Instagram: jsal_motivates.
Email: scrubies@optimum.net.
Feel free to also email me! This is my personal email.

CPSIA information can be obtained
at www.ICGtesting.com
Printed in the USA
LVHW030623090121
675849LV00006B/829